MW01108919

ABOUT LIFE!

by Jerry E. Tobias

This book contains original and general statements only.
No other person was intentionally or knowingly quoted.

Copyright © 2006, 2008 by Jerry E. Tobias

Published in Omaha, Nebraska USA by FACTORS PRESS
P. O. Box 541236, Omaha, Nebraska 68154-1236 USA
For information or orders, contact Info@FactorsPress.com

ISBN 9780970058249

Library of Congress Control Number: 2005938739

First Printing 2006
Second Printing 2008, revised

To Carolyn

*my precious wife, best friend, and faithful
and encouraging companion, who has walked
with me through the years and the events
and experiences of life that have been used
to teach us both the principles in this book*

>>>>>>> · <<<<<<<

FOREWORD

The following is a portion of a work that I wrote for my family when I was first diagnosed with cancer. These pages reflect the principles that I believe should define and guide our lives, especially concerning our relationships, our purpose and our priorities.

My desire in putting these things on paper was to encourage those close to me to review the principles that govern *their* lives and to reassess what is important - and what is not - as they train and prepare for eternity.

I hope that you will consider these same issues.

Jerry E. Tobias

The LITTLE RED BOOK ABOUT LIFE!

Living for God's purposes and glory
is more important than
anything gained by living for self.

A good hug is initially
more important
than good advice.

How you live your life
is more important than
what you do for a living.

The impact of your life
is more important than
the length of your life.

*The attitude with which you approach
a difficult situation is more important
than the difficulty of the situation.*

The high priority things that don't demand
your attention are more important
than the low priority things that do.

The principles you live by
are more important than
the positions you hold.

Having a great marriage
is more important than
having a great job.

How kind you are
is more important than
how clever you are.

How much you understand
is more important than
how much you know.

Character
is more important
than charisma.

Having a pure heart
is more important than
having a pleasant appearance.

How you treat those who can't do anything for you is more important than how you treat those who can.

*Laughter is more
important for the soul than
liniment is for the body.*

How you impact your family
is more important than
how you impress anyone else.

*Having a purposeful life
is more important than
having a prosperous life.*

People
are more important
than possessions.

22

What you model
is more important than
what you proclaim.

The commitment made
is more important than the
inconvenience it may have created.

*Knowing the One who holds
your future is more important
than knowing your future.*

How those around you rate your
character is more important than
how banks rate your credit.

The decisions ahead of you
are more important than
the decisions behind you.

The content of your heart
is more important than
the capacity of your mind.

The significance of what you do
is more important than
the size of your paycheck.

Being honest
is more important than
making a good impression.

*Preferring others
is more important than
protecting yourself.*

*Commitment
is more important in marriage
than compatibility.*

The people involved in the endeavor
are more important than
the outcome of the endeavor.

33

The strength of your faith
is more important than
the severity of your problems.

Being respected
is more important
than being rich.

How thoroughly you consider the consequences of a decision is more important than how quickly you decide.

*Integrity and a servant attitude
are more important in leadership
than experience or management style.*

Being a good listener
is more important than
being a good speaker.

*Making a difference
is more important than
making a fortune.*

That which lasts forever
is more important than
that which will soon be gone.

*Having your children's respect when
they are thirty is more important than
having their agreement when they are ten.*

Any person
is more important
than any thing.

A heart at peace is more important
for your health than
a handful of prescriptions.

The time that you give your children
or grandchildren is more important
than the toys that you give them.

*Your word
is more important
than your wealth.*

Having a good attitude
about the day is more important
than having a good day.

How well you finish
is more important
than how well you begin.

*Dependability
is more important than
natural ability.*

Resolving the problem
is more important than
assigning the blame.

Having your character tested and strengthened is more important than having a life of ease.

Tenacity
is more important
than talent.

51

*Avoiding unnecessary debt
is more important than
acquiring unnecessary things.*

The effort made
is more important than
the success achieved.

Having a compassionate heart
is more important than
having a clever mind.

*The content
is more important
than the packaging.*

An obedient attitude
is more important than
a compliant response.

*Principles
are more important than
power or prestige.*

*Understanding
is more important
than agreement.*

What you do with the gifts and talents
you have is more important than
what gifts and talents you have.

*Being your children's parent
is more important than
being their pal.*

*Having a loving and inviting home
is more important than having
a large and impressive office.*

Finishing life with good relationships
is more important than
finishing life with great wealth.

The respect you earn
is more important than
the authority you are given.

The valuation of your character
is more important than
the valuation of your estate.

Doing the right thing is more important than the cost or consequences of doing it.

The lives you affect
are more important
than the things you collect.

A few words of encouragement and understanding are more important than volumes of reason and logic.

The wisdom you leave your family is more important than any wealth you might leave them.

What is really in your heart
is more important than what
others may think is in your heart.

*Your spiritual condition
is incredibly more important than
your physical condition.*

The relational value of a meal
together is more important than
the nutritional value of that meal.

The days ahead of you
are more important than
the years behind you.

The things in life that aren't
things are more important
than the things that are.

Listening to those who don't agree with you is more important than listening to those who do.

*A simple gift given out of love is more
important to the recipient than an
expensive gift given out of obligation.*

How well you receive advice
is more important than
how well you give it.

*Being thorough
is more important
than being fast.*

How much glory God receives
is more important than
how much credit you receive.

Honesty and integrity
are more important than
accomplishments or success.

*Effort
is more important
than intellect.*

*Patience
is more important than
the pace of progress.*

81

Being rightly related
is more important than
being right.

How well your children behave
is more important than
how cute they look.

83

The laughter in a home
is more important
than the luxuries.

How well you have treated others
is more important than
how much you have achieved.

Listening with your heart
is more important than
listening with your head.

*Perseverance
is more important
than strength.*

Your family
is more important than
television or technology.

Meaningful relationships
are more important than
meaningless things.

The time you spend WITH someone
is more important than
the money you spend ON them.

Reliability
is more important
than resourcefulness.

Maintaining integrity
is more important
than "getting ahead."

Learning to serve
is more important than
learning to lead.

How you spend the years you have
is more important than
how many years you have.

94

An unnoticed life that is lived for others
is more important than
a highly visible life that is lived for self.

What you LEARN from an experience
is more important than
what you EARN from it.

The size of your heart
is more important than
the size of your home.

Generosity
is more important
than genius.

How completely you have forgiven
is more important than
how deeply you have been hurt.

*Respect
is more important than
reward or recognition.*

The significant things gained during difficult times are more important than the insignificant things that are lost.

*The path traveled
is more important than
the speed of the journey.*

*Hearing what you need to hear
is more important than
saying what you want to say.*

How well you do something
is more important than
how many people see you do it.

Relationships
are more important
than riches.

How much you learned
is more important than
how much you enjoyed the process.

Things that really matter
are more important than
things that really don't.

Attitude
is more important
than aptitude.

How giving you are
is more important than
how gifted you are.

Parenting
is more important than
any profession.

How willingly you follow
is more important than
how well you could lead.

Behavior
is more important
than brilliance.

The beauty of the rainbow
is more important than
the inconvenience of the rain.

Your reputation as a person
is more important than
your rank or your status.

114

Being there for your family
is more important than anything
you have to miss to be there.

Maintaining the relationship
is more important than
winning the argument.

Anonymous acts of kindness
are more important than
public acts of generosity.

Whether or not you forgive
is more important than whether
or not you receive an apology.

*Giving children the boundaries they
need is more important than giving
them things they don't need.*

Trusting God
is more important than
understanding the problem.

The words in your note or letter
are more important to the recipient
than the quality of your penmanship.

The people impacted by the plan
are more important
than the plan.

The value of the help given
is more important than
the cost of giving it.

Having a peaceful home
is more important than
having a prosperous business.

How you choose to treat your peers
and subordinates is more important
than how you have to treat your boss.

How well you respond to the unexpected is more important than how well you manage the planned.

*Your actions
are more important
than your intentions.*

Your personal values
are more important
than your valuable things.

Consistency
is more important
than capacity.

How honest you are
is more important than
how eloquent you are.

How much you have shared with others
is more important than how much
you have accumulated for yourself.

*Your private behavior
is more important than
your public image.*

132

*Guarding your heart
is more important than
guarding your treasure.*

The purpose of the process
is more important than
the speed of its completion.

How well you care for those close
to you is more important than
how well you captivate the crowd.

The motive for the action

is more important

than the action.

Building up your family
is more important than
building your fortune.

Availability
is more important
than ability.

The depth of your follow-through
is more important than
the speed of your commitment.

Consistent private encouragement
is more important than
occasional public praise.

Doing the right thing is more
important than whether or not
anyone ever knows that you did it.

A child's character development
is more important than his
physical or academic development.

The humility you maintain

is more important than

the honors you receive.

The sincerity of your words
is more important than the skill
with which you deliver them.

Being prepared for eternity
is more important than
being prepared for retirement.

The long-term impact
is more important than
the short-term gain.

Spiritual strength
is more important than
physical stature.

Your character
is more important than
your credentials.

Your attitude about life
is more important than
your age or physical condition.

Treating people well
is more important than
achieving power or position.

Honesty is more important than ANYTHING *gained through or protected by deception.*

How you are thought of by the
people who know you is more important
than how many people know you.

A person who needs you
is more important than
a project that can wait.

*Faithfulness
is more important
than fame.*

*The Word of God
is more important than
the opinions of men.*

*How grateful you are for what
you have is more important
than what you have.*

*Your level of integrity
is more important than
your level of authority.*

How much your life honors God
is more important than how often
your lips may speak of Him.

The people affected
are more important than
the profits gained.

How interested you are in others
is more important than
how interested they are in you.

*The opportunity to encourage
someone is more important than
the effort that it may take to do so.*

What is really true
is more important than
what appears to be true.

*Understanding the character of God
is more important than understanding the
challenges and uncertainties ahead.*

How much you know about things that matter is more important than how much you know about things that don't.

How genuine you are
is more important than how
polished you appear to be.

How freely you give
is more important than
how much you have to give.

The motives of your own heart
are more important than
your assessment of others' motives.

The love, affirmation and encouragement
you give your family are more important
than the things you may give them.

Your relationship with the Lord
is more important than
your status among men.

The lives you have touched
are more important than
the tasks you have completed.

Maintaining your health
is more important than
increasing your wealth.

The principles violated in order to win are more important than the prizes that may have been won.

*The motive for giving
is more important than
the size of the gift.*

*Taking time to determine
the truth is more important
than acting quickly.*

*How teachable you are
is more important than
how talented you are.*

Your attitude about something you MUST do is more important than your attitude about something you'd really LIKE to do.

How considerate you are
is more important than
how creative you are.

The amount of wisdom you accumulate is more important than the size of the fortune you build.

*Small things done with genuine
concern are more important than
big things done with ulterior motives.*

*Your choices
are more important than
your circumstances.*

How much what you do or say
honors God is more important than
how much it impresses men.

THE *MOST* IMPORTANT THING

This book is about purpose, priorities and people. However, it is impossible to have real purpose, meaningful priorities or right relationships without knowing God, *the One for whom we were created and for whose glory we live.* God, though, is Holy, and our unholy lives (sins) separate us from Him. But He loves you and me so much that He sent us His only Son, Jesus, who - by His sinless life, death (the penalty for our sins) and resurrection - sets us free from sin so that we might dwell in God's presence both now and eternally. When we respond by *repenting* (turning from our sins and forsaking the right to run our own lives) and *believing* (trusting in and totally committing our lives to Him), God forgives *all* of our sins, puts His Spirit within us, and guides us through all of life's triumphs and trials.

To understand more about *your* relationship with the Living God, visit StepUpToLife.com. Address additional questions or comments about this book to the publisher, or to Contact@TheLittleRedBookAboutLife.com.

FACTORS PRESS
OMAHA, NEBRASKA USA

ABOUT THE AUTHOR

JERRY TOBIAS is a pilot, author and speaker who lives in Omaha, Nebraska. He flew everything from small aircraft to Boeing 747s during a thirty-eight-year career as a U. S. Air Force, missionary, corporate and airline pilot. He has written for numerous professional aviation periodicals and spoken internationally as an aviation safety and human factors specialist. He also speaks to church, corporate and civic groups.

Jerry has been married to his wife, Carolyn, for forty years, and has two grown children and two grandchildren. He is also a cancer survivor.

Jerry can be reached at Contact@TheLittleRedBookAboutLife.com.